TANTRUMS
AND
TEMPERS

TANTRUMS
AND
TEMPERS

Tried-and-tested ways of helping
your child cope with strong emotions

Dr John Pearce

THORSONS PUBLISHING GROUP

First published in 1989

© DR JOHN PEARCE 1989

British Library Cataloguing in Publication Data

Pearce, John, 1940 Oct. 27 –
Tantrums and tempers.
1. Children. Home care – Manuals – For
parents
I. Title II. Series
649.'1

ISBN 0-7225-1721-1

Illustrations by *Willow*

Published by Thorsons Publishers Limited, Wellingborough,
Northamptonshire NN8 2RQ, England

Printed in Great Britain by Richard Clay Limited, Bungay, Suffolk

1 3 5 7 9 10 8 6 4 2

CONTENTS

To Mary

INTRODUCTION

Most people think of anger as a nasty and unpleasant mood that is best avoided. It certainly can be very unpleasant and destructive, but anger can also be creative, constructive and sometimes even enjoyable! Anger that is well directed and still under control can get things changed for the better and motivate people.

This book looks at the way in which anger, in its various forms, develops in children and in families, and considers effective ways of managing a powerful and potentially damaging emotion. Parents probably have more difficulty dealing with their children's angry and aggressive behaviour than any other aspect of upbringing. This is partly because anger can show itself in so many different ways and partly because children can provoke their parents to feel the most extreme anger themselves, which at times can be quite overwhelming.

To be angry towards your own child is a very uncomfortable feeling because the expected and more usual emotion is one of love and caring. In fact the emotions of affection and anger, loving and hating can occur together in the same person at the same time, even though they work in opposite directions. Anyone who is a parent or who looks after children, will have to cope with these powerful mixed feelings.

One way of coping is by understanding what is going on. In other words, understanding where the anger came from, what caused it in the first place and why it takes a particular form. However, childcare is not only to do with understanding. To understand is not so difficult because there are so many possible explanations for what causes emotions and most of them will seem to fit equally well. No, the really difficult bit is dealing with the strong feelings in both yourself and your child and channelling them into a positive force for change and improvement rather than a force for destruction and distress.

The many different forms that anger can take are covered in this book and there are questions and answers to help you clarify the main issues. The most important part of the book is the section on practical management. This part can be read on its own and is based on methods that have been well researched and found to be effective – even for the most difficult children.

This book, however, is not just about difficult or dis-

THE EMOTIONS OF AFFECTION AND ANGER CAN OCCUR TOGETHER IN THE SAME PERSON AT THE SAME TIME....

turbed children. It is about 'normal' children and day-to-day problems that are not major, but nevertheless take up your time and energy and can even build up into a big problem if allowed to continue.

You may ask, 'Why do parents need to read a book on coping with children, surely it is better to follow your own instinct and do what comes naturally?' This approach still works for many parents, but nowadays instinct seems to be less reliable, perhaps because we have become too intellectual about bringing up children. Maybe there is too much advice, too many TV and radio programmes (and even too many books!) on bringing up children. Another factor is that more parents than ever before have to cope with the care of their child on their own. Not only are there more single parents, but the support of grandparents and other relatives is less likely to be immediately available due to increased mobility and separation of family members.

There is yet another problem that parents face: which of the many approaches to childcare should they adopt? How are they going to decide which method works the best? Of course what usually happens is that one method is tried and if that does not work, then another is attempted . . . and another . . . and another. In the end any parent will be inclined to give up or give in, leaving a child who is confused about what is expected and what is right and wrong.

In recent years there have been great advances in the understanding of the nature of emotions and family relationships and this in turn has led to much more effective ways of dealing with problems that occur in everyday life. Unfortunately this knowledge is not easily available, mainly because it comes from many different sources and is therefore difficult to bring together in an effective way, but another factor is that childcare is strongly influenced by fashions and there is a tendency for parents and others to follow the latest trend without looking for the evidence to support it.

Like most other writers of guidebooks for parents, I have based the book on a combination of research evidence and practical experience with my own children. However, in addition to this, my everyday work is with the most difficult, disturbed and complicated children. This has been helpful in making the advantages and disadvantages of each approach very clear to me. I can therefore be confident that what I recommend here will work if you apply it consistently and stick at it without giving up.

You may think that I take a rather firm line that could cause children to become upset, but if you read the book carefully you will find there is always a good reason for being tough. You must remember that love and indulgence are not the same thing. Indeed, more trouble is caused by parents giving in 'for a quiet life' than for any other reason. It is not easy to stick to what you have said and to what you

WHEN I SAY THAT I WANT YOU TO DO THIS **NOW** I **MEAN** IT....

WELL, AT LEAST I **THINK** I DO....

OH.... FORGET IT... MAYBE ITS NOT SO IMPORTANT AFTER ALL....

IT IS NOT EASY TO STICK TO WHAT YOU HAVE SAID....

believe is right, especially if you are not sure that you are doing the right thing in the first place.

It is my hope that you will find most of the contents of this book 'common sense'. If this is the case you should be even more confident in the way you manage your children and, at the same time, know more of the theory behind the practice. If, on the other hand, you disagree with what I say, this does not matter, provided your own method is working well. However, it is important to remember that it is easy to get away with mistakes when children are young, because young children are remarkably tough and forgiving. The same cannot be said about adolescents, who are easily upset and, given half a chance, will put the blame on you, even if this is totally unfair!

I would like you to feel that I am talking directly to you as you read through the book. You can 'talk' back to me if you don't agree with what I am saying or if you don't understand. Then read on and it should become clear why I have taken a certain line rather than any other. Don't hold back from having an argument with me in your head or asking someone else what they think. In this way you will become much clearer about what you believe yourself.

Childcare is not so much about right and wrong, but more about finding the best compromise between the various demands of family life. For this reason it is impossible to 'get it right' all the time and, as a parent, this often leads to feelings of guilt. In fact, an inevitable part of being a parent is feeling guilty about not doing the right thing for your child!

Most parents are not extremely indulgent, hardhearted, strict or inconsistent (at least, not for long!) In extreme cases it is easy to see that something is wrong, but it is in the middle ground where there is the greatest scope for discussion, disagreement and debate and, of course, guilt.

If you are unsure about your own ideas, but have some reservations about what I have written, I would like you to follow my suggestions as closely as possible. I have been very careful to give guidelines and advice only where I am confident that it is safe, reasonable and effective. If you have followed the guidelines and they have not worked, don't immediately think that I have got it all wrong. It is much more likely that you are not sticking closely enough to what I have said. So, read it again, have another go . . .

and don't give up!

Please remember that if I recommend a particular way of dealing with a problem that seems to be very tough and potentially upsetting for your child, this is because I know that it is effective and does no harm to a child. Young children need firmness and structure in their lives in order to give them a feeling of security. In fact, being tough and firm in setting limits on children's behaviour is one way of showing them that you love and care for them.

It is the love you have for your child that makes being a parent so fulfilling and full of joy. But, it is this same bond of affection that makes it so painful and distressing when things don't go right. Our feelings of love vary from time to time and fortunately it is not necessary to love your child all the time in order to be a reasonable parent. However, children do need to be cared for and protected from harm. This may mean that you will have to be very firm and decisive and be prepared for your child to be upset and angry because he or she can't get his or her own way.

At the end of the book there is an appendix outlining some of the research on anger and tempers for those of you who would like to have more detail and to read further on the subject. I hope that there is something to interest everyone, even if you have no children. After all, we were all children once and anger is a mood we all experience.

CHAPTER 1

UNDERSTANDING TEMPERS AND TANTRUMS

Tempers and tantrums are difficult to ignore, unsettle everyday life, are unpleasant to watch and may even be dangerous. Most of us would be happy if our children only occasionally became angry, rarely had a temper and never had a tantrum. However, it is important to remember that it is quite normal for young children to go through a phase of having tantrums. There could even be some cause for concern if your child doesn't show signs of anger as he or she grows older.

Children vary a lot in the ways they show their anger, depending on many different factors. These can include:

- the child's temperament
- family expectations
- the child's sex
- cultural background
- the child's age and stage of development
- family communication
- the child's physical and emotional state
- social factors

The various causes of tempers work together a bit like watercolour paints: you start with red and yellow, mix the two together and you have three different colours – red, yellow and orange. Add a third colour, like blue, and you have a whole range of colours. This is called an 'Interactive Relationship' where the interaction of individual factors produces more causes than the separate factors alone.

Although each of the main groups of causes is mentioned separately here, it is important to remember that they all react with each other in this complicated way. If you want to know *why* your child has a bad temper, you should be able to work it out from what follows, but don't look for a *single* cause. It might help to make a list of every factor you can think of and then give each one a 'contribution' score from 0-10 so that in the end you will have a better idea about what is causing your child's tempers, if there is a pattern to them, and what you might be able to change. You could also get another adult who knows your child well to do the same and then compare results.

Tempers and temperament:
the difficult child

'Temperament' is used to refer to the way a child will generally react to situations and to the usual way it behaves and shows emotions. The temperamental characteristics combine to form the personality, which gradually becomes more clearly formed as the child grows older. Even at birth, though, children have different temperaments and, in fact, there is evidence that a large part (may be as much as 80 per cent), of our temperament is inherited. You only have to look at newborn babies in the nursery to realize how different they are from each other.

At birth some babies are placid, easy and predictable in their behaviour, while others are restless, difficult and unpredictable. Often it is possible to recognize the temperament of a baby even before birth, by its activity level and responsiveness to what is happening to the mother. Differences in behaviour and emotions are therefore largely 'constitutional', that is, how the person is made. This does not mean that what happens in the child's environment is not important – quite the opposite. It is the finishing touches that make all the difference.

One way of looking at personality is to think of it as being rather like a picture. A child is born with a certain type and size of canvas, brushes and a unique personal set of colours, which, to some extent, will decide the make-up of the child's personality. In the end it is the person's life experiences that will make up the final picture, although this will be limited by what they started out with.

THE FINAL PICTURE WILL BE LIMITED BY WHAT THEY START OUT WITH....

It is increasingly recognized that some babies are born difficult. The so-called 'Difficult Child' is easy to recognize because he or she has the following characteristics right from the start:

- **unpredictable** – usually difficult to feed, to put to bed or to toilet and then sometimes easy
- **very strong emotions** – usually having tempers and crying, rather than being happy

● easily disturbed by change – slow to settle and difficult
to comfort.

If you happen to have a child with a difficult temperament
you will immediately recognize these characteristics. You
have a tough time ahead of you but don't despair. There
are things that you can do to help your child and many
children will have grown out of it before they start school.
Of course, lots of children would fit into the description
given above, but it is possible to distinguish between
children who are *born* with a difficult temperament and
behave in this way right from the start and other children
who have been allowed to *learn* how to get attention and
get their own way by being difficult.

Children who have a difficult temperament that is
present from birth have a much higher rate of problem
behaviour and tempers than easygoing children. They are
also more likely than other children to have cuts that
require stitching, which is just one sign of how serious the
problems really are! Children with a difficult temperament
also require 'extra super' parenting if they are to be
helped, so it is not going to be easy. They need more of the
following than you would normally provide:

● routine and regularity
● clear limit setting
● high level of supervision
● firm, consistent discipline
● frequent comfort and reward.

If you are able to provide this extra care, most children will
learn to modify their temperament reasonably well by the
time they start school, but some children will continue to
be difficult and then it is just a case of carrying on with the
guidelines above with determination and increased inten-
sity.

The guidelines above should be helpful for any difficult
child, but you will have noticed that there is a strong

emphasis on regularity, consistency and firmness. This is hard work for anyone and it will also be hard for your child. If you have decided that your child needs this type of help, it is most important to balance the rather controlling form of care with a great deal of positive care and love. Otherwise you will find that you are forever getting at your child and saying things like, 'stop it', 'be quiet', 'come here', 'don't' . . .!

You may find it difficult to be loving towards a child who has lots of tempers and is frequently irritable and disobedient, so you have to work at it. Here are some ways of balancing all the negative experiences that your child will go through if he or she has a difficult temperament.

- Try and avoid situations that you know your child is going to be unable to cope with without being very difficult and temperamental. These occasions only give your child practice in how to be difficult and annoying! However, if it is something like getting dressed in the morning or going to the toilet, you obviously can't avoid it. In this case a regular routine is helpful, so that your child becomes used to doing things automatically, and knows that arguments and tempers are pointless.
- Look out for any good thing that your child does, especially if he or she manages to control temper in a satisfactory way and give lots, tons, gallons, heaps, oodles of praise. Don't worry about going over the top with your praise, it is difficult to give too much.
- Set up situations that you know your children should be able to cope with without losing their tempers even though they may not get their own way. This gives them practice in temper management and gives you a time to give praise rather than telling them off again.
- Arrange special times when your child is alone with you or another adult, purely to enjoy the time together. This is 'high quality time' and many times more worthwhile than being together in the ordinary way,

DOING SOMETHING THAT YOU BOTH ENJOY.....

when you have something else to do at the same time, for example the cleaning or making a meal.

Many parents use 'high quality time' without really knowing what they are doing – it just seems the natural thing to do. With a difficult child, though, you have to think things out and work hard at it for it to have any effect. Here are some guidelines for getting the best from this special time:

- do something that you both enjoy, such as a game, playing outside, going for a walk, or just talking
- make sure that there are no distractions (like the TV) or disturbances (such as other people coming into the room)
- it is best to keep this special time short and intensive so that you both finish feeling that you would like to do it again – five minutes of high quality time every day or

every few days may be quite sufficient and better than many hours of ordinary time.

This special time reminds children that they are indeed special themselves and that what they do is important to you. In other words you are showing that you care for your child and love him or her, even if you have to be firm and tough at times.

Tempers and temperament: the easy child

Some children are amazingly easy to bring up and rarely, if ever, have a temper or tantrum. Although this could be due to your being a wonderful parent it may also be that you have a child with an easy personality who has none of the characteristics of the difficult temperament. But there are other possible reasons for a child not having much of a temper, such as:

- an anxious and sensitive child will tend to avoid getting angry, because it is too upsetting. This child needs to learn how to be angry without it getting out of control. It might be a good idea to have a joke about how to be angry and get the child to practise being cross
- some children who are very slow and backward in their development are rather quiet and passive. If this is the case, the delay in development will become more obvious as the child grows older. There are lots of things that can be done to improve their skills but not much that will change their ability level
- if you are a very strict and restrictive parent, your child will not dare to show his or her temper (but may do so when you are not present). It is worth thinking about this possibility if you get reports of your child

having lots of tempers when away from you, but when at home he or she behaves perfectly

- it could be that you are too easygoing and indulgent. If you give in to every wish of your child it is possible to avoid tempers and tantrums for quite a long time . . . but not forever!
- perhaps you have done a good job and helped your child to manage his or her temper very well!

Family expectations

Each parent has certain expectations of how their child should behave and any parent would be happy if these expectations were met all the time. Life is much more complicated than this, because children often have other ideas and so do other relatives and friends. However, the standard of behaviour that parents set is important in guiding the child to understand what is acceptable and what is not.

There are a number of influences that affect the way parents develop their own expectations of acceptable behaviour and it is useful to know what they might be:

- there is a very strong tendency to repeat your own childhood experiences of parenting with your child
- if your parents were either too strict or too soft with you, you will have a tendency to counteract this and go too much in the opposite direction with your own child
- if you think your partner is too strict or too soft, this will also make you likely to counterbalance this and swing too much the other way
- the religious, social, political and national culture you have adopted will probably affect you more than you would care to admit
- your own personality will obviously play a part in what you are prepared to put up with
- your age will also make a difference: young parents tend to be rather too soft and easygoing and elderly parents usually have high expectations of good behaviour
- parents probably have higher expectations of their first child and lower standards for their youngest child
- most parents also have different expectations for their daughters and their sons: on the whole, boys are able to get away with more aggression and tempers than girls – yes, even these days!

It is remarkable that children (and even teenagers) tend to follow their parents' wishes and opinions on most major issues, provided that the parents' views are clear and consistent. Where this is not so, the children are more likely to 'do their own thing'. If both parents can agree on what they expect from their children and they make this very clear, then the children will know exactly where they are and eventually most of them will fit in and conform.

These family expectations take a while to build up and develop into a 'family tradition', but this can become a very strong and influential force, particularly if the family is a large one. Equally this influence of the family can be undermined by grandparents or other family members who have other ideas.

Building up a family tradition is an effective way of getting your child to behave and conform, without having to say too much yourself. If your family tends to argue and show aggression, don't be surprised if the children do the same, they are only conforming and keeping to the family tradition!

Ask yourself, 'What expectations and traditions have I got in my family'. If you are not sure, then this will also be the case for your child and you might be better off if you established some. It will need a lot of careful discussion and thought. Don't be put off if you are on your own or if your partner is uncooperative – in some families it is left to one parent only to decide these issues, and this can be successful even if it is much harder work.

These expectations and traditions lead to the family developing it's own style or way of coping. Some families will show little anger, while others may accept anger and tempers as a normal way of getting what you want. There is little evidence that either approach is better than the other and, provided there is consistency and agreement between the parents, it would only be in extreme cases that there might be a problems.

Do boys have more tempers than girls?

Yes, boys do indeed have more tempers than girls. They are also more aggressive and show more anger. This certainly fits with what most people would expect, which in itself may be the main reason for this difference. In other words there are different standards of behaviour for the two sexes and boys live up to the expectation that they are more aggressive than girls. Generally parents, particularly fathers, play more rough and tumble, 'mock fights' with their sons and behave differently towards them from an early age.

The difference between boys and girls tends to increase as they become older. This could be due to increasing social pressures to behave in an aggressive way or there could be other influences at work. Although baby boys and baby girls may appear much the same in their behaviour at birth, boys are more vulnerable or 'at risk' than girls right from the start:

- there are many more miscarriages of male than female foetuses
- at birth there is a difference of about a week in maturity with boys being more delayed
- this immaturity of boys continues and increases so that by eight years of age there is a difference of a year that increases to two years by puberty (males never catch up – at the other end of life there is still a difference and females live five years longer than males)
- more boys are born with some form of handicap than girls
- more boys die in the few weeks before and after birth, but, to 'compensate' for this, more boys than girls are born
- all developmental problems such as bed-wetting, soiling, speech and language difficulty, clumsiness, reading and spelling problems and hyperactivity, are all more common in boys
- boys have a higher rate of psychiatric problems than girls, even though in adult life it is females who suffer more frequently.

It would be impossible to explain these differences purely

in terms of social influences and it is clear that there are strong biological or constitutional factors that make boys more vulnerable than girls. It is likely to be this biological immaturity, as well as the effect of social attitudes, that leads to an increased frequency of tempers and aggression in younger boys.

Also, one possible explanation for this increased vulnerability in boys is that they have less chromosomal or genetic

material than girls, since they are missing a leg of the X chromosome:

$$Female = XX \qquad Male = XY$$

It is thought that the female's extra genetic material has a protective and controlling influence on the other genes that is absent in boys. There is some suggestion that the Y chromosome itself may have an influence on aggression and tempers. This is because some research showed that people with one or more extra Y chromosome were found to be more aggressive than normal. Recently, however, there has been some doubt about this.

There is another important biological influence in older boys. This is the effect of the hormone testosterone, which begins to increase its production about two years before there is any physical sign of puberty. It is well recognized that high levels of testosterone in either animals or humans, lead to increased muscle power and a raised level of aggressive drive. It is interesting to note that testosterone also increases in girls at puberty, but the increase is much smaller than in boys.

In spite of these very real differences between boys and girls in the frequency of angry behaviour and tempers, which have both a social and a biological basis, most of the variations between individuals are caused by other influences and not just by being male or female.

Cultural influences on tempers and anger

Quite apart from the factors within the individual and the family that affect the way anger is dealt with, there are also wider influences that come from outside the family. Some Asian cultures have a strong tradition of not showing anger. For example, Burmese children are taught to smile and be pleasant even if they are feeling frustrated and angry. Sikh children are taught to be humble, which means controlling feelings of resentment and anger against others.

Not only are there differences between national cultures, but there are also variations within cultures from time to time, rather like a pendulum swinging. For example, the suppression of anger was seen as a desirable quality in Victorian times, but in the Last 50 years or so in most Western cultures there has been an increasing move towards 'free expression' of feelings. This has had far-reaching effects on the standards by which children are brought up. However, it looks as if people in Britain think that the culture of free expression has gone far enough and they are now keen to push the pendulum back the other way a bit!

Religion plays an important part in many cultures in setting the moral standards by which families run their lives. The reduced influence of religion in many Western societies and the misuse of religion by terrorist organizations has resulted in a weakening of moral values. To some extent the State also sets standards with the 'laws of the land', but these laws are only applicable at the extremes of behaviour and hardly deal with the important issues of personal loyalty, honour, responsibility, relationships and caring. It is therefore not surprising that many parents are unclear about their own moral standards and that their children often have difficulty distinguishing right from wrong.

If your child asks you, 'Why is it wrong to have a temper tantrum?', ideally you should have an immediate answer that is convincing for you and seems right. Here are some possible answers:

- temper tantrums upset other people
- God does not like tantrums
- tantrums are unacceptable in our family
- grown-up people don't have tantrums
- tantrums make things worse for you
- it is wrong to force your will on other people
- people won't like you if you have tantrums
- tantrums will get you into trouble.

None of these answers are completely right or satisfactory. There are many other things that you could say, but it is important that you have thought about it and you have worked out your own values. If your child is not able to get his or her standards of behaviour from you then they will get them from somewhere else which may not be so acceptable!

Stages of development

Very young babies cry, go red in the face and seem to be

angry, but it is often not clear what all the fuss is about and, even later on, it is not unusual for a child to cry for no apparent reason. Gradually, as the child becomes more mature, the crying and the associated behaviour is more obviously a temper.

Tempers reach a peak frequency around two years of age and, in some ways, they are at their worst then. Hence, this stage is sometimes called 'the terrible twos', but the age of the child is not as important as the stage of development. If your child is immature or slow in development then the temper stage will be reached later and last longer.

At two years of age, about 20 per cent or one in five children have tempers that are regarded as a problem by their parents. At this stage two to three tempers a day, lasting five to ten minutes, would be within the normal range and even an occasional temper lasting for longer is not necessarily abnormal at this age.

The reason for the frequent tempers around the age of two is related partly to problems that a two-year-old has in communicating, but another important reason is that two to three years of age is the time when children first become aware of themselves as individuals. They start referring to themselves as 'me' rather than by their name and later 'I' rather than 'me'. This increasing awareness of the Self is also seen when children recognize themselves in photographs without someone else pointing them out. Also, between two and three years of age, children looking in a mirror recognize themselves and, if they have a dirty mark on their face, they will rub it off their own face rather than rub the mirror. Thus, children at this stage of development become aware of their own identity and their individual needs.

By five years old, 10 per cent of this age group still have problem tempers but it would not be abnormal for a five-year-old child to have an occasional temper lasting 10 minutes or so and to have one to two tempers a day lasting for a few minutes only. At 10 years of age, many days should be free of tempers and any tempers that do occur should last only a few seconds, but may occasionally last up to five minutes.

As tempers become less frequent they also change in character. The violent first stage of the temper gradually gets shorter, but the sulking second stage grows longer, until during adolescence, when tempers once again become more numerous and sulking and brooding is common.

Most two-year-olds have tempers that are caused by conflict with the parent when they are told that they must not do something. Arguments over toileting are also frequent, followed later by tempers over dressing. By five years old, many of the tempers are directed at other children and concern joint play. Of course these are generalizations and each individual child is different, but it will give you an idea about what most other children are doing.

Family communication

Communication is a very important part of tempers, because they are a clear and sometimes dramatic way of letting people know that an angry person is not getting what they want and they are distressed about it to the extent that they are prepared to upset others. For this reason it is very rare for tempers to occur in private. If you put a child with a temper tantrum in a room on it's own, either the temper will stop or the child will increase the amount of noise it is making to be sure that you can hear. Occasionally children in a temper will do something really devious or destructive to make absolutely sure that your attention is focused on them.

Tempers occur most frequently at the stage of development (about two years old) when children have a good understanding of the meaning of many words (200 words at two years old), but still have some difficulty in putting the words together into sentences. As a result, communication can be frustrating for them and it is easy to misunderstand what they are trying to say.

Children with communication problems due to deafness, language problems or slow development are more likely to have tempers for the reasons outlined obove. Partial deafness is very common in young children, and it is often associated with infections of the ear, nose and throat. It is easily missed and difficult to test for. If you are in doubt, it is best to get your child's hearing tested professionally and, if you are still doubtful, then ask to see a specialist.

Deafness owing to infections may vary from time to time, which can cause a lot of confusion. It may help to develop your own test, like whispering something your child would normally respond to, for example, 'It is time

for bed' or 'Would you like an apple?' Or, you could use the tick of a clock or watch and move it slowly away from your child's ear and note the point at which the tick is no longer heard. Make sure that you cover the other ear while doing the test. When you have noticed the distance of the vanishing point of the tick you should then do the same test with somebody who has normal hearing and compare the two results. Both these tests can be easily made into a game and are good fun for children, but they will only give you a rough indication of your child's hearing.

Speech and language problems are associated with tempers and difficult behaviour. Speech problems include stammering and all forms of unclear speech, while language problems involve a more complicated disorder of the understanding and organization of words. Sometimes the disorder of language is very subtle and only affects one aspect, such as the expression of language where the child understands but can't find the right words to communicate with. Not surprisingly these children easily become frustrated and angry. As with most developmental delays these problems are more common in boys than in girls.

Parents may also have communication problems that can occur in several different forms:

- the 'Double Message' is a common problem of communication: the parent says one thing but seems to mean something else – for example, the instruction, 'Go to bed' is said with a tone of voice and a smile that says, 'I am not really serious about this' or, to give another example, 'I am not having any bloody swearing in this house'
- some parents are keen that their children should understand exactly *why* they have to do something and so give long and complicated explanations, but, unfortunately, many children stop listening after the first minute or so and they are left more confused than they were before
- inconsistent communication is a problem for all parents and is one of the most frequent causes of anger, resentment and tempers for both parents and their children – parents may say contradictory things at different times or in different places, they may also be inconsistent in what they say to different children, but the most disruptive form of inconsistency is when parents disagree between themselves and have different standards for their children's behaviour
- unclear speech is quite rare in adults, and children quickly learn what their parents mean if the words are given a strong emphasis and are accompanied by clear gestures
- deaf and dumb parents will obviously have difficulty in communication, but their children quickly learn to communicate and develop normal language themselves and, interestingly, deaf children of deaf parents often develop better communication skills than deaf children of normal-hearing parents
- a parent whose mother tongue is different to that of

their child may have problems in communicating with their child depending on what language is spoken at home and how proficient the parent is at speaking it, but, once again, much will depend on how good the parent is at using gestures and their tone of voice

In addition to these problems there are other more subtle forms of family communication difficulties, for example:

- **'The Family Secret':** the parents have a secret that they wish to keep from other people, but their secretive and guilty behaviour alerts the children that something is not quite as it should be. The children may then imagine that something must be badly wrong and become emotionally unsettled, which, in turn, may lead to tempers
- **'The Stiff Upper Lip'** family who don't show their feelings and try and avoid people getting upset at any cost, will generally have children who also don't show when they are angry and, all may seem to go well, but angry feelings may come out in other ways (often as physical symptoms) or they may suddenly explode and give everyone a terrible shock
- **'The Family Myth':** although there are many possible myths, one that frequently affects tempers in children is the linking together of two family members because they are thought to be the same, for example, 'Johnny has his father's temper' or 'Jenny takes after her great aunt Sally who was well known for her bad temper' – clearly this makes it difficult for the child *not* to have a temper!
- **'The Family Label':** here a child gets a label that is difficult to change even if the child wants to – 'The Angry One' or 'The Defiant One' will encourage the child to have tempers and be difficult
- **'The Family Style':** this is perhaps the most subtle form of communication of all and yet it is very influential. Each family develops its own way of

dealing with stressful situations and coping with anger and usually this is not spoken about, it just happens. Obviously it is the parents who set the tone and the children fit in and follow what their parents do – for example, some families argue a lot, talking in an aggressive way to each other and the children copy this style of communicating, which may work well within the family, but, outside the family, there are likely to be misunderstandings and the children will be thought to be aggressive by normal standards. Usually, neither the child nor the parent are aware of any problem because it is part of their everyday life.

The child's physical and emotional state

Sick children tend to be more irritable and have more tempers. Parents compensate for this by being indulgent and giving in to their child's wishes to avoid any distress. It is important to do this while the child is unwell, but as the child gets better, it is sometimes difficult to change.

Children with chronic or life-threatening illnesses are particularly likely to get stuck in an irritable state. Parents feel that they have to be careful all the time and will give in rather than upset their child or risk a temper tantrum. Unfortunately this usually makes the child very demanding, temperamental and not very nice to be with. If your child has been ill, you should look out for this risk as he or she recovers.

Obviously if your child is acutely ill, he or she will benefit from your care and indulgence, but at some stage you will have to return to normality otherwise your child might decide it is rather nice being spoilt and given into and find they can control you and get their own way by threatening to get upset and having a temper.

There are hardly any conditions where a short period of upset would be harmful for your child, provided that you are just doing what you would normally do. In fact, by being normal you will actually reassure your child that things are not too terrible. Or, put the other way round, the more you indulge a sick child the greater will be their anxiety that the illness is serious. Even if this should be true, it is helpful for seriously ill children to remain optimistic and as normal as possible, so they should be *treated* as normally as possible.

Tempers are more likely to occur when a child is hungry or tired. You can therefore expect them before meals and later on in the day. A common time for irritability and tempers occurs when a child returns from the nursery or school because they will be both tired *and* hungry. Fortunately, both these problems are easily dealt with and it is a good idea to provide a snack and a quiet time as soon as your child returns home (it might also be effective for the parent who is irritable on arriving home from work!)

Children who are under emotional stress for any reason at all are more prone to irritability, tempers and aggression. Sometimes it can be difficult to tell that your child is under stress because children (and adults) tend to try and pretend that the stress isn't there in the hope that it will go away. Irritability and tempers that come out of the blue and are unexpected are therefore a useful sign that your child is experiencing stress and that they are having a problem coping.

Social factors

We have seen how tempers and disruptive behaviour are associated with factors that relate to the child such as personality, age and sex and factors that arise within the family such as attitudes, communication and expectations. There are also more general social factors that are associated with tempers and behaviour problems as follows:

- living in the town or city is linked with an increased rate of tempers. The reason for this is unclear, but it is likely that there are many different stress factors that occur more often in areas of dense population—for example, poor housing, overcrowding, unemployment, broken homes and lack of play space
- lack of a father figure increases the risk of tempers, particularly in boys. This may be due to the fact that discipline is more of a problem for a single parent, or emotional disturbance following the loss of a father or identifying the child as being difficult, 'just like his father' – the same being true, of course, if the father is the single parent but with the loss of the mother obviously being the cause of the disturbance
- large families seem to have more arguments, but you might expect this because a family of two can only

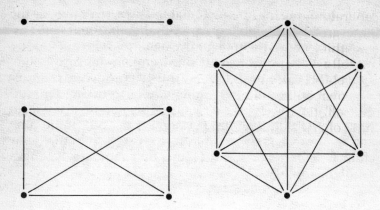

Possible arguments with different combinations of family members – the more family members, the more possibilities there are

argue with each other, a family of three has three combinations of people to argue with, a family of four has six chances and a family of six has 15 possible arguments they can have with different combinations of family members!

- mothers who smoke heavily are more likely to have a child with temper tantrums, but the reason for this is not clear. It could be that these are mothers who are under stress with many adverse circumstances to deal with, but there are many other possible explanations for the association between cigarette smoking and tempers
- children who live in the North and the Midlands are also supposed to be more likely to have tempers – goodness knows why!

Conclusion

Although a lot is known about tempers – when they occur, what causes them, who has them and so on – this is very general knowledge that has been gained from studying large groups of children. It is interesting and tells us something about the mechanisms of tempers, but it does not tell us about individual children – about your child. Each child is unique and if you want to know what causes your own child's temper you will have to work it out for yourself, taking into account all the factors that you can think of as I've outlined them above.

CHAPTER 2

HOW TO COPE WITH TEMPERS AND TANTRUMS

Even the most placid child will become angry at times. In fact it is normal for children to go through a stage when they show anger frequently and with little provocation. Children's anger is almost always related to not getting what they want for themselves. So, it is not surprising that tempers are especially noticable at the time when children begin to see themselves as separate individuals. This happens around the age of two to four years.

Loving and caring are opposite to hate and anger, but they can occur together in the same person at the same time, which can be very confusing! All parents naturally use their feelings of loving and caring to counteract any hateful, angry feelings that either they or their children might have. So, the more you are able to help your child to be loving and caring, the less likely it is that the child will be angry and have tempers. But, that said, it is not simply a case of loving and caring for your child enough and everything will be all right. Life is much more complicated than that! Each child has separate and unique needs, which are changing all the time. On some occasions it may be necessary to be very tough and firm with your child, which can also be a way of showing your love for your child. It is surprising how frequently children say, 'I wish my parents would be firmer and stricter with me'.

There are many ways of loving and caring for a child, but one of the less obvious ways is to teach a child self-control. Helping a child to learn how to deal with their own anger

and tempers is part of the development of self-control. Children who have learned how to control and manage their emotions and behaviour in a reasonable way, will also have developed self-confidence and good self-esteem.

Teaching a child how to be angry

Children have to be taught how to express their anger appropriately. Some parents do not allow their children to show any anger at all and teach them by being very repressive and cross every time the children are angry or aggressive. This approach may work for a few years and a very docile child would result, but eventually the child would probably copy the angry behaviour of their parents and become cross and aggressive themselves.

Other parents get very hurt and upset every time their child becomes angry and take their child's anger as a personal attack. Eventually the child comes to fear the power of their own anger and therefore suppresses it. Later on this may lead to the child being inhibited, anxious and passive.

A few parents, however, take little notice of their children's angry outbursts and even laugh at them. If this approach is carried on for a long time the child will have difficulty learning how to control its temper.

Most parents try several different approaches when dealing with their children's anger, tempers and aggression. This can also cause problems because it may be difficult for the children to know what their parents really want.

Should parents 'teach' their child how to be angry? It may seem a strange idea, but if you do nothing, it will probably be other people who do the job for you. Obviously there are 'good' ways of being angry and not so good ways. Here are some ideas about 'good' ways of being angry:

- the anger is a response to something that *most* people would find unacceptable
- the anger is expressed immediately
- the angry reaction is in proportion to the seriousness of the cause
- the anger is under control, rather than the other way round where the anger controls the person
- the anger does not last much longer than the event that caused the angry feelings
- relationships are not permanently damaged by the anger.

Here are some of the common problems caused by being angry in the wrong way:

- bottled up, suppressed anger will sooner or later cause problems
- anger that builds up and gets out of control can be damaging and frightening
- unexpressed anger may get misdirected, when it comes out at a later stage
- uncontrolled anger spoils relationships.

Clearly, it is important to teach children how to manage their own anger in such a way that they don't have these problems, but they are able to express anger effectively.

Perhaps the best way of teaching children how to be angry is to show them by example. Easier said than done, but here are some ideas:

- tell your child when you are feeling angry, so that they know what is going on and what this emotion is all about
- try not to lose control of your own temper. If you are going to get angry, then it is best to 'do it' early on, before things have got out of control. If you are angry in this way you might even be able to enjoy the experience!
- explain to your child what is making you angry, using simple words only
- tell your child what you plan to do to put things right
- be prepared to apologize if you feel you have gone 'over the top'.

It is certainly difficult for anyone to behave like this, but at least this is something to aim for!

Remember that most children's moods do not last as long as adult's moods. They can come and go in a few minutes, so it is worthwhile 'cashing in' on this and making sure that you don't keep the mood going on longer than necessary by being angry and bloody-minded yourself.

It is also worth remembering that the more frequently your child has a temper that goes out of control the more it will become a habit. In fact, after each temper your child will become that much better at throwing a tantrum – until he or she is really expert at it!

Prevention is better than cure

Parents often spend a lot of time working out what is the best way of dealing with tempers and tantrums. There is a danger that the focus gets fixed on stopping children doing things. It is much better instead to concentrate on what you would like your child to do.

If you want to concentrate on getting children to do the right thing rather than spend most of your time and effort stopping them from doing the wrong thing, then you must make it very clear exactly what it is that you expect. This may sound obvious, but it is amazing how often children get confused or double messages from their parents. Here are some examples of unclear messages:

- parents may say something quite firmly, but the smile on their face suggests that they are not serious
- a mother may be keen for her child to be gentle, but the father encourages the child to be aggressive by play fighting and encouraging the child to fight and beat other children
- a child may be told off for being rude and then laughed at when they are rude about someone the parents don't like
- one child in the family may be allowed to have tempers and get away with it, so the others also expect to be able to have tempers
- parents who have different expectations on various occasions or are unpredictable, will not give a clear message to their children about how they should behave.

Part of being clear is being consistent and saying the same thing over and over again, but this is not so easy because there are so many other things to do and think about. However, it is really worthwhile working hard at it and making sure that you are not being undermined by the attitudes of your partner or any of your friends and relatives.

Most parents make a very good start at giving clear messages to their babies. For example, when a baby does anything good, the child receives a lot of praise and encouragement. Babies are frequently told how much they are loved in a very clear and obvious way. Unfortu-

nately parents tend to give up this clear communication after a while – perhaps they become tired out or they think the child should know what is expected without the parent having to say. If children are left with any doubt in their minds about what they should do they will do what they want to do whatever it is the parents would like.

A good example of misunderstanding a message is the partially deaf child who is able to hear when a sweet is offered, but seems not to hear when it is bedtime or the washing up has to be done!

If your child doesn't take enough notice of what you say, then try going back to the clear communication you gave when your child was younger. Give extra-clear communication and be extra pleased when the child does what you want. Don't be put off if there is no immediate response. If you feel that you have got it right and can't think of any way of improving things, then just keep at it and don't give up. If you have got it about right, you should see things beginning to change after about three weeks and definitely improved after three months. If there is no improvement you should consider the following possibilities:

- whatever it is that you are doing, you are not doing it quite right. Try reading the book again! Discuss anything that is not clear with a friend, and see what they think
- your efforts are being sabotaged by someone contradicting what you have been saying and doing
- you are doing all the right things, but just not being clear enough about it. It pays to put a lot of effort in over a short period to get things right. Afterwards, life is much easier!
- your child has a difficult temperament and will need much more clear and persistent instruction than other children
- perhaps now is the time to get professional help.

Avoid situations that cause tempers

It is often possible to predict which situations are likely to cause your child to become angry and have a temper. For example, when you tell your child that he or she cannot have a sweet or a toy they ask for. Of course, sometimes it is impossible to avoid these situations, but here are some suggestions that are worth trying:

- don't give your child toys or sweets frequently or regularly (apart from present-giving times such as birthdays and Christmas). Giving sweets regularly after school or when you go out anywhere will set you up for having to give sweets, crisps or drinks in order to avoid an outburst of temper. Not much fun, and quite expensive after a while!
- children are more likely to have outbursts of temper when they are tired or hungry, so watch out for 'danger times', before meals and at the end of the day. *But* take care not to give food just to keep the peace or you will end up with a pudding-shaped child. Rearranging mealtimes and bedtimes may be all you

have to do, or giving food and rests in smaller amounts more frequently

- a common time for tempers is immediately after an event that has been exciting or tiring, such as returning home after going out, or being picked up from the nursery or school. Plan this time in advance so that you can spend time calming the child and providing extra attention

- when your child has been away from you, even for a few hours, it is a good idea to spend time re-establishing your relationship. One way of doing this is by each

TELLING EACH OTHER WHAT YOU'VE BEEN DOING

telling the other what they have been doing during the separation. If you always do this, your child will eventually get into the habit of telling you things and will enjoy it – even demand it! Talking to each other in this way sets things up for good communication between both of you later on, when it may be really important

● when you are away from home, especially when you want your child to be on his or her best behaviour, tempers are more likely to occur – children seem to know when they have more control over you than usual! They know that you are more likely to give into their demands when in public. It is consequently advisable to keep these times short, pleasant and as much under your control as possible. Try and keep your child occupied and gradually increase the time in public. If you have a set-back and things get out of control, don't panic, just go out for a shorter period next time and gradually build up again

● one of the most difficult situations is when you are with relatives, particularly your own parents. Remember all the points above, but, if things go wrong, don't let relatives interfere, unless it is at your request. They usually make things worse! Tell them that you know what you are doing and that you expect them to back you up.

Never be blackmailed by tempers

As soon as children realize that they can get what they want by having a temper or even threatening to have one, you have got a problem. If you give in, you are training your child to become an expert in blackmail! If, on the other hand, you stand firm and don't give in, you may also be treated to a temper. But, at least if you stand firm you will be less likely to be threatened in this way in the future and your child will eventually learn that having a temper does not help to get what he or she wants or to win friends.

When do children learn to manipulate you in this way? Much earlier than you might think. Even small babies learn to manipulate their parents by their crying and tempers. It is quite helpful to remember that manipulation of other people to get your own way is a very primitive and basic skill. It therfore needs to be brought under control reasonably early on so that the child can become socially skilled. The sooner you start this training the easier it will be. Older children who are manipulative (and for that matter adults too) are unpleasant to be with and they generally become isolated, unhappy and lonely people.

Of course most parents use blackmail themselves at some time or other, saying, for example, 'I will get cross if you don't stop behaving badly' or 'If you do what I say and you are a good boy, you will get a sweet'. This teaches children all about blackmail and they become rather good at it themselves! You may find it better to be positive and clear and say things like, 'I want you to behave well and this is what I expect you to do . . .' Then be very clear and say exactly what it is that you want them to do.

It is so easy to give in for a quiet life, but this only stores up problems for the future that most of us could well do without. It really is worthwhile being firm and then having the pleasure of seeing this pay off later when your child shows good self-discipline and gets what he or she wants in an acceptable way. It is an important point to remember that self-control and self-discipline have to come from outside first. Children are not born with much in the way of self-control and the only way children can develop this ability is for their parents and other adults to provide it for them until they have learnt how to do it themselves. In this way children gradually learn how to manage their own wishes, desires and feelings.

Give distractions and warnings

If you see your child working up to a temper, it helps if you can get in quickly and distract the child, but this will only work if you intervene early enough. Watch out that your distractions are not just another form of blackmail in disguise or your child will soon learn to work the system— just threaten a temper and along comes an interesting distraction!

If you see a child heading straight towards a temper, it is easier to gently steer the child off course rather than to go off in a completely different direction, which usually requires a major distraction that may be seen as a reward for threatening a temper.

Here are some simple examples of distractions that you can try:

- getting the child to do something helpful is a good idea because it is difficult to have a temper and be helpful at the same time! For example, a child says, 'I want my meal now!' and you respond 'Yes, just help me lay the table' or 'Let's go and have a look at the clock and you can help me see if it is teatime yet . . . Oh look, it is 3

GIVING A RUNNING COMMENTARY ON WHAT IS HAPPENING AROUND YOU CAN OFTEN PREVENT A TEMPER FROM DEVELOPING....

o'clock, it is time for . . . (whatever you have planned to do)'

- giving a running commentary on what is happening around you can often prevent a temper from developing. 'We are just going to cross the road now and we are looking both ways to make sure nothing is coming. Look at the boy on the bike. Is it clear now? Off we go then. Listen to the noise of the lorry. Here we are on the other side. Which way are we going now?' Because you are going on and on and on, the child will usually be distracted from moodiness and tempers

- asking questions will sometimes work. The child stops to think of the answer and, because it is difficult to concentrate on two things at once, there is a good chance that the moodiness will be forgotten, at least long enough for the child to be distracted

- many parents find it helpful to use toys as a distraction. Make sure that they are easily available, so that you can immediately provide the distraction before things get out of hand and early enough for the toy not to be seen as a reward for threatening a temper.

Giving a warning to your child can be helpful in preventing anger and tempers building up and getting out of hand. Do be careful to give a warning that can be carried out easily otherwise your child will quickly learn that you don't really mean what you say. Here are some examples of warnings that are difficult to carry through or make things worse in other ways:

- 'If you have a temper I will smack you'
  There are three problems here:
  1 smacking is likely to teach a child how to be physically aggressive
  2 even if you feel that smacking is acceptable, it is difficult to carry it out in public because other people are likely to make comments

3 smacking usually makes tempers worse rather than better

- 'I will tell your father if you have a temper and he will punish you when he gets home'
  The problem with this type of warning is that the result is too delayed and probably unpredictable, because the father may not feel like being angry and punishing the child
- 'I won't let you out to play for the whole day if you have another temper'
  This type of warning can be difficult to keep because it means having a rather fed-up child at home all day. Children quickly learn that if they moan and groan and are difficult enough when being kept in, then most parents will relent and let them out, just to have a bit of peace and quiet. Also, strange as it may seem, some children actually enjoy being indoors
- 'If you have a temper you won't be able to have a sweet'
  Although this may work once or twice, most children will soon learn that they can get a sweet very easily, just by threatening a temper.

But don't be put off by these disadvantages. It is helpful to be aware of the problems so that you are less likely to make the mistakes that all of us make at times. There are many advantages of giving a warning and here are some of them:

- a warning makes it clear what you want from the child
- it tells the child what the consequences are of not doing what is expected and what has been asked
- when the consequences happen it makes more sense to the child
- you will feel better because you are doing what you said you would do, rather than being pushed by your child to do something on the spur of the moment and then regretting it afterwards.

Perhaps the most important thing about giving a warning

is to be sure it makes sense and if it is linked to a threat, that you are prepared to stick to it. So why not try some of the following suggestions:

- 'If you carry on like that there will not be enough time left to play a game with me'
- 'If you don't stop by the time I count three I will leave the room'
- 'If you continue like that you will be so tired you will have to go to bed'
- 'I am leaving the room until you have stopped all that noise'
- 'If you want to do something nice (that you have already arranged) then you had better not have a temper'
- 'If you think you are good at tempers, wait till you see me get into one!'

IF YOU THINK YOU'RE GOOD AT TEMPERS, WAIT TILL YOU SEE ME GET INTO ONE!

Each warning uses a slightly different approach. Every child will vary in his or her response to warnings, depending on temperament and the situation. It is obviously important to carry out any threat you make, otherwise you won't be taken seriously. Sometimes children get used to the warnings and take little notice. So it is a good idea to vary them from time to time.

Sometimes it can be more effective to use a joke warning. This works partly by being different and therefore more noticeable, but joke warnings also work because it is not easy to laugh and be angry at the same time. An added advantage is that if you like your own joke it will help you to keep your cool. Here are some examples of joke warnings just to give you an idea of what you might say if you can't think of anything yourself and to show you that it is not necessary to be a brilliant comic:

- 'Watch out! Stamping your foot like that is hurting the floor. Did you hear it cry out just then?'
- 'You are not shouting loud enough. Please stamp your foot harder and shout louder . . . No, louder than that . . . No, even harder! . . . Is that the best you can do?'
- 'If you shout any louder the penguins in the South Pole will hear you'
- 'Your stamping is making the house shake . . . I hope the roof does not fall in'
- 'You sound like a parrot when you go on like that.'

Obviously joke warnings can make things worse, but at least it is under your control, and the joke, however pathetic, often changes the focus of the anger. A joke warning can also be a way of showing the child that you are not very impressed with the temper and you are not going to take it too seriously.

Expect an apology

If all your efforts at trying to prevent the temper have been unsuccessful, *don't worry!* You are in very good company. Every other parent has had the same problem! There is still a lot that can be done to help your child after the temper has finished.

When the temper is over it is helpful to expect your child to apologize. This signals the end of the anger and helps the child to carry on normally rather than going on sulking. The temper is put in the past and the child is able to make a new start. An apology also helps to re-establish good relationships and to put things right again after the outburst.

IT IS NOT IMPORTANT FOR THE APOLOGY TO BE SAID IN THE RIGHT TONE OF VOICE....

It is not all that important for the apology to be said in the right tone of voice or with a great feeling of remorse. The main reason for the apology is to help the child to learn that it was wrong to have a temper and to allow the anger to get so out of control. The apology helps to make things right again after being angry and it is a good idea for an adult to apologize if they themselves have been too angry and gone over the top. This teaches children by example.

Making up after an argument or outburst of temper is very important for everyone concerned. It teaches children how to finish an argument without finishing the relationship, which is obviously an important skill to learn before adulthood.

Remove all attention and isolate

In spite of all the good intentions and plans, things don't always work out as you would like them to. Sometimes, whatever you do seems to have no effect or may even make things worse. Maybe you are not feeling too good yourself or your child is particularly determined to be bad tempered. What then?

Have you ever noticed that children rarely have an outburst of temper when they are on their own? Temper tantrums are performed for an audience. So if you leave the child in a temper, even if he or she is screaming and kicking on the floor and walk out of the room, the temper will be unlikely to carry on much longer.

Removing attention from your child can be very difficult if the child is causing damage or injury. If you feel it is too risky just to leave the child where it is, then you will have to remove your child to where it is safe. The bedroom is often the safest place for a child to be on it's own, but some parents feel it is wrong to use the bedroom because it should be a comfortable place. However, the most important reason for using the bedroom is because it is safe and the child can be left there without attention for a few minutes.

Time out

The procedure of removing attention and isolating is

sometimes called 'Time Out', which is a technical term for isolation from any attention or reward. It should be carried out on a carefully scheduled basis. The Time Out procedure involves identifying a specific unacceptable behaviour and then immediately removing attention in a predetermined way whenever this behaviour is observed.

Quite a lot has been written for parents about how to use Time Out. The Americans are especially keen on it. There are two main varieties of Time Out that parents can use:

- **Time Out in a separate room: here the child is removed from the situation in which they are behaving badly and sent or taken to a room where they will get no attention. The child is then left there for a specific number of minutes**
- **Activity Time Out: here a child is not allowed to join in a particular activity, but is not removed from the situation. the child is still able to see the activity going on.**

The period of isolation is timed by the clock and is usually for a few minutes only. One minute per year of age would be a reasonable guide. The Time Out is then repeated as often as is necessary to have the desired effect. There are many problems in using this rather rigid way of coping with tempers. The name 'Time Out' gives the impression of a technical procedure and is sometimes used to describe an extreme type of prolonged and total isolation that is not appropriate for a family home. Some children actually prefer to spend some time away from the situation that has been causing them to be angry. In this case the Time Out is a reward and will have the reverse effect of that intended. Other children resist the Time Out and their temper escalates. This may then lead to increased attention being given to the child, rather than less. Finally, Time Out teaches children what they should *not* do, rather than what they *should* do.

Star charts

Star charts and records can be a helpful way of keeping a check on a child's behaviour so that both you and your child can be more aware of what is happening. A 'star chart' is one particular form of record where the day is divided up into separate parts. If the child has no tempers during any one period, a star is put on the chart to show

I'M DOING **MUCH** BETTER ON MY **GOOD BEHAVIOUR STAR CHART** THAN DADDY IS ON HIS, ARE'NT I MUM?....

that the behaviour was good. if the child has been bad then the chart space is left blank or is marked with a cross. Instead of stars you can use ticks, smiley faces, little drawings or anything else that appeals.

The idea behind a chart is very simple and may seem artificial. However there is more to a chart than you might think.

- the stars become rewarding in themselves
- the chart tells the child and the parent about progress and improvement
- the focus is changed from the bad behaviour to concentration on good behaviour
- a chart can reduce the arguments between a child and the parent by acting as a common goal
- a chart diverts attention and anger away from people and onto the chart
- a chart helps parents to be more consistent
- the chart acts as a record of exactly what is happening
- a chart can help communication between parents and also between parents and children.

The chart should be divided into periods during which it is possible for the child to be well-behaved and not have a temper, at least on a good day – so that it is not too difficult to gain a star. As soon as you feel that your child has got the message, the stars need to be made a bit more difficult to achieve. This can be done by gradually increasing the duration of each period.

Children between the ages of five and twelve years usually respond well to charts, but they are not much use for younger children, apart from acting as a record to inform parents of progress. It is important to make the chart into something special and interesting and to involve the child in the organization of the chart as much as possible. Try and make it good fun and something for your child to be proud of.

One of the most difficult things with a chart is to keep it going and keep the motivation going as well. You will need all your ingenuity to keep up your child's interest in the chart. Here are some ideas:

- put the chart in a prominent position such as on the kitchen or living room wall
- involve other family members or friends in praising the child for any success

- get the child to try and achieve progressively more stars in a row (i.e., a longer time without a temper)
- give the stars a value, e.g., 1p per star, or five stars gain the child a privilege such as staying up a bit later for one night, having a story read or playing a game
- don't make the stars worth too much otherwise it can get right out of hand!

Most charts work well for a day or two but then things slip back into the bad old ways unless you work hard to keep the chart interesting. Aim to have the chart for a fairly short time such as one to four weeks. If things are no better by then, something is wrong somewhere and you should think again about what is going on. Possibly this is the time to consider getting professional help.

Although a chart will be a record of your child's progress, you may find it helpful to keep your own private diary of the behaviour. You can then make notes on exactly what it was that caused the behaviour and a blow-by-blow account of what happened. After a week or two you may see a pattern emerging that will show you what is going on and will give you ideas as to how to change things to improve the behaviour.

What about allergies?

Most parents would like to have a simple explanation for why their child is moody and has tempers. There is the hope that a simple cause might have an easy solution. Allergies to food and food additives is just such a case. In fact, single, simple causes of tempers and anger are very rare in children. However, the food allergy theory has great appeal and has become very fashionable. The truth is that, although food allergies are not uncommon in young children, there is very little evidence to link them with mood and behaviour disorders. Many of the tests for allergies are at best unreliable and at worst totally false and misleading. Tests done on hair and skin are the most unsatisfactory because they tell you little or nothing about what happens when the food is eaten and digested.

The concern about food allergies and additives is now so widespread that a few facts might be helpful here:

- the link between food and allergic reactions isn't new, it has been well recognized for many years. Recently, however, a much wider range of foods and additives have been blamed for a vast range of symptoms
- the main foods that can cause allergies are: shellfish, milk, eggs, wheatgerm (gluten) and, less frequently, other cereals and fruit
- the additives that cause by far the most frequent allergic reactions are related to azo dye colourings, and preservatives such as benzoic acid and sulphite derivatives
- some other foods, like chocolate, tea, coffee and, of course, alcohol can produce reactions in the body, but these reactions are not allergic. They are caused by substances that can produce a response in anyone if taken in large enough quantities, although some people are more sensitive to them than others
- the most frequent symptoms of food allergies are: rashes, tummy aches, diarrhoea, nausea and dizziness, but don't forget that any of these symptoms could be caused by a large number of other things
- although a lot of research seems to indicate that allergies to foods or additives could cause behaviour disturbance, hyperactivity or learning problems in some cases, better-controlled research tends to show that there isn't a link but, as yet, there is no conclusive evidence either way
- any person who is tested for food allergies is likely to show a reaction to several different substances. This is especially so with young children, where every child will normally have positive results even if they do not suffer from obvious food allergies

● if a food or additive gives a reaction to a skin or hair test, it does not necessarily mean that the person is going to be allergic to the substance when it is eaten in an everyday diet.

The only way to be sure that food allergies are causing problems is to have a diet where the suspect foods or additives are removed completely. After two weeks on the 'exclusion' diet one substance at a time is re-introduced every two weeks. A detailed record of symptoms must be kept during this time and this is best done by someone who does not know what the diet consists of.

If there seems to be a reaction to the added substance then it should be removed again without the child or diary keeper knowing, just to make certain that it really is having an effect. The reason for all this secrecy is that it is very easy to believe that a particular food is causing symptoms when in fact it isn't. The symptoms of food allergies are very non-specific and can be produced by a number of physical and emotional causes, so it is easy to get confused.

If you think a particular food is causing tempers or moodiness, it is worthwhile experimenting a bit. Exclude the food or additive for two weeks and then give it again and note the effect. Even if the effect is very dramatic it is advisable to try the food again to see if the problems return and it was not just chance that improved the tempers. Try asking other people if they have noticed any difference. If it works that is wonderful. However, if you remove some foods from your child's diet, watch out for nutritional deficiences. If you are in any doubt at all, get expert advice from a doctor or dietitian.

One important reason why an exclusion diet may be helpful is that parents are usually very firm about it and the child learns that the parent is in control and that it is no good making a fuss or having a temper about food. The children benefit from this lesson and learn how to keep better control of their tempers.

When it all falls apart!

If all else fails and the temper gets right out of control, you may have to hold your child. Never attempt to hold a child in a temper unless you are sure that you are strong enough to be in total control. Holding a wriggling bundle of anger

HOLDING A WRIGGLING BUNDLE OF ANGER IS NOT MUCH FUN FOR YOU....

is not much fun for you, but could be great fun for the child if it becomes clear that you are losing control and he or she is winning the 'contest'.

Most parents would find it fairly difficult to hold down a child on their own when the child is aged five years or older. It all depends on size and strength, but think carefully before you tackle an older child (who, in any case, should have grown out of tempers by that age).

Holding a child in a temper is a high-risk business! There is a risk that either you or your child will get hurt and almost certainly the temper will get worse before it gets better. There is no way of telling when is the best time to hold a child, except to say that it is when the parent feels it is right. This technique is not right for every child or every parent, but it can be extremely helpful in some cases.

Here are some step-by-step guidelines for holding a child in a temper:

- your child must be out of control or nearly so
- you should feel that holding is the right thing to do
- give your child a warning so that he or she has a chance to regain self-control
- warn other people what you are planning to do
- sit the child on your lap, facing away from you so that your face cannot be seen and so that the child does not get extra attention
- put your arms around the child's middle and, with your left hand, hold the child's right wrist. Then, with your right hand, hold the child's left wrist
- now cross your child's arms over so that your arms are uncrossed. To do this you will have to pull firmly but only hard enough to keep them in position on either side of the child's hips
- your child's legs should be between your legs, which should be crossed at the ankles so that you can grip the child's legs firmly enough to prevent them thrashing around
- when your child wriggles and struggles, you should tighten your grip just enough to control the child and prevent an escape. When the child calms down you can relax your hold. But don't leave go and be prepared to tighten your grip if there is another struggle or wriggle
- once you start holding your child it is important to see it through to the end – when your child has calmed down either through exhaustion or because it is clear

that you are determined to be in control and the child realizes that there is no point in continuing in a temper

- you will have to continue the hold for as long as it takes, which may be minutes or hours
- one possible way of bringing the holding to an early end is to tell the child to be still while you count up to five and if they are still you will let them go. However, it is generally best to talk as little as possible to your child during the holding
- finally, make sure that your chin is not near the back of the child's head in case you are knocked out with a backwards head-butt!

Well, it sounds rather like all-in wrestling and very complicated. Holding a child in this way is better than being pushed into a temper yourself or going over the top and smacking or beating your child. This holding method works by showing your child that you are in control and that you can safely cope with his or her anger. In the end your child will not only feel more secure and safe, but will also have learned something about self-control. This type of holding is not for everybody, so only use it if you feel comfortable and confident about it.

CHAPTER 3

UNDERSTANDING ANGER AND AGGRESSION

What is anger?

Anger, perhaps more than most emotions, is self-centered and selfish. It occurs when someone is unable to have what they want, when they want it. An angry emotion may also develop if a person feels that there is a threat that they will not get their own way. So when a child is told that it can't have an ice-cream even though the ice-cream van is playing its jingle and other children are having ices, an angry scene often follows. The boy is angry and wants to have the ice-cream immediately. He won't be satisfied by being told that he can have one tomorrow. The parents, on the other hand, are angry as there is a threat that they may not get what they want, which is to have a reasonably obedient child. Anger is therefore strongly bound up with a person's ego or selfishness and is driven by a primitive and basic desire to have personal needs satisfied.

The word 'anger' comes from the Latin 'angere', meaning 'to strangle', which sounds pretty bad! But anger is more often used as a very general and broad term, which ranges from mild irritability at one end of the spectrum, to violent aggression at the other. Tempers are somewhere in the middle, with tantrums being further up the scale towards all out aggression. The word 'aggression' comes from the Latin 'aggredi', meaning 'to attack'. It implies that a person is prepared to force their own will on another person or object even if this means that physical or psychological damage might be caused as a result.

Compared with most other emotions, anger is a fairly simple and straightforward feeling, but it can combine with other moods to make up more complicated emotions such as jealousy or grief. For example, jealousy includes the following feelings: anxiety, anger, hate, fear, misery, hopelessness and frustration. It is unlikely that anger ever occurs entirely on its own as a single mood state. Anger is normally accompanied by anxiety, possibly because there is always a chance that the angry person's wishes will not be met and they won't get what they want when they want it. Certainly it is a common experience to feel very anxious when being angry. It can be a rather disconcerting experience to feel really angry, but at the same time to feel so panicky, anxious and shaky that it is difficult to express the anger clearly.

The link between anger, aggression and other emotions

The association between anger and aggression is obviously a close one. What differences there are depend more on semantics than anything else. Most people would see aggression as a more extreme form of anger that has a strong physical component. But we also use the word aggression to describe the emotional drive that athletes have in order to do well, which does not involve much in the way of anger. However, there is a link between these two meanings of aggression, which is that both aim to put another person or competitor down in an inferior position.

Of all emotions it is anxiety that is the most commonly experienced. It is even more common than anger. There is a very close connection between anger and aggression and anxiety and it is important to understand the nature of this relationship. An emotional reaction occurs as a response to a stress, which may be caused by an event outside a person, such as being told you can't have an ice-cream, or by an event inside the person, such as the thought, 'I think my parents love my sister more than me'.

Whenever a stressful event occurs, the first feeling to be experienced is anxiety, which explains why it is the most frequently occuring emotion. If the stress is mild then there is unlikely to be any progression onto other emotions, but if the stress increases, sooner or later anger will develop. An example of this would be a child who is jealous of his sister and is under stress in situations where he could be treated unfairly. When he sees his mother get a bag of sweets out he becomes anxious that he won't have

his fair share and watches carefully, anxiously counting out the sweets. If the sister is indeed given more sweets than him, his stress becomes greater and he may then become angry and aggressive. So, where there is anger you should expect to find anxiety as well. You will see this in yourself when you are angry – do you remember the anxious feeling, the shaking and the 'butterflies in the stomach' feeling that occur when you are angry?

The physical and psychological symptoms are much the

same for anger as they are for anxiety, although they will tend to be rather more severe in states of anger and aggression. It can sometimes be very difficult to tell whether a child is angry or just very anxious, because the behaviour can be so similar. For example, a boy with school phobia will become increasingly anxious as he gets closer to school. Eventually he may develop quite aggressive behaviour in his attempts to avoid going to school, even though the reason for this is his worry about being able to cope in school.

If the stress continues to increase, the anger and anxiety will also increase until eventually a state of depression and misery may result. It is often the case that a temper will end in tears and, in our example of the jealous boy, he too may finally become withdrawn and feel miserable and unloved if he is continually made to feel jealous and angry. Once again the physical symptoms of anxiety and anger are also the same for depression and misery and you should always expect depression to be accompanied by both anger and anxiety.

The development of anger and aggression

If a baby does not arrive in the world crying and making a lot of noise, we become worried, but it is very difficult to know exactly what emotion the baby really is experiencing. It could be anger and resentment at leaving the nice warm womb or it could be that being born is a very uncomfortable process that makes the baby cry in pain. It is not until a child is a few months old that it is possible to be sure that anger is the mood that is being expressed rather than a much less specific form of distress. Gradually, children become more able to express anger and get into a temper until during the second year they become very skilled at it! It is at this time that tempers reach the peak of frequency and the expression of anger is well developed, but yet to be controlled or 'tamed'.

Aggression deliberately directed against another person does not really show itself before the age of 18 months but becomes more obvious over the next few years. Tempers, on the other hand, actually tend to become shorter, but the effects of any violence become greater as the child becomes bigger and stronger. So aggression develops more slowly and reaches a fully developed stage (but not necessarily controlled) some time during adolescence. As the anger and tempers are brought more under control the time spent brooding and sulking usually gets longer, so it may seem as though the temper is going on for longer as the child grows older even if this is not really the case.

In the first two years, most of the anger and tempers arise as a result of conflict with parents – first over toileting and doing dangerous things and later over tidying away toys and dressing, but the precise nature of the tempers will vary from one child to another. By the age of five years a larger number of arguments are with other children rather than with parents and the children frequently turn to aggression and fighting as a way of resolving disputes.

The socializing effects of school play a significant part in reducing the frequency of tempers. The child comes under the influence of other children and adults who don't make the same allowances for bad behaviour as may happen at home. From school age onwards, tempers are mostly confined to the home and involve those who are nearest and dearest.

Conclusion

Anger and aggression are very closely linked together and also with other emotions. The link with anxiety is a particularly close one. All emotions develop stage-by-stage as the child grows older and it is helpful to know something about this in order to be able to work out the best way to understand and cope with your child's tempers and tantrums.

CHAPTER 4

TEMPERS AND TANTRUMS: QUESTIONS AND ANSWERS

These questions and answers are organized into two parts. The 'Yes but . . .' section is for parents who maybe do not fully agree with what I have said. They have got their own ideas, which are, or at least seem to be, different from mine. The 'What if . . .' section is for parents who generally agree with what I have said but can see all the problems and pitfalls.

Yes but . . .

'My child is very placid and never seems to get angry'

Children vary a lot in temperament and it is quite possible for a child with an easy-going temperament to experience very little anger. On the other hand, anxious and sensitive children may not show much anger because it frightens them, but they feel anger strongly and quickly sense it in other people. If a child is a slow developer he or she will be delayed in reaching the stage when anger and tempers become obvious. In the slow developer there will be little sign of anger and tempers until the child has reached the developmental stage of a one-and-a-half to two year old.

'My child has terrible tempers even though he is now six years old'

Tempers and bad behaviour are more common in boys than girls, but you would expect a child to have a reasonable control of their temper by the time they start school at the age of five years. At six years of age a temper should not last much longer than a few minutes or occur more frequently than once every few days. It is difficult to be more specific because tempers are so dependent on the circumstances in which they occur. However, if your child is still having frequent or very bad tempers after starting primary school, there must be something wrong somewhere. It may not be serious, but it needs to be dealt with. The longer a child continues to have tempers, the more difficult it is to change.

Here are some reasons why bad tempers might not improve as your child gets older:

- **your child has a difficult temperament: if this is the case the child will have been difficult from birth – if not before!**
- **you have not been able to be firm enough in helping your child to gain control of tempers and anger**
- **you have been inconsistent in your response to anger and tempers, so the child has not been able to learn how to manage anger**
- **the child has witnessed a lot of anger and tempers in the family and has come to believe that expressing anger is the best way of getting what you want and being noticed**
- **the child has got into the habit of having a temper as soon as a feeling of frustration develops. The angry response habit is both automatic and unnecessary, but very difficult to stop.**

'I think that all children should express their anger freely'

It is a common notion that it is good to express anger, but it is not as easy as that. If children are allowed to express their anger freely and without any check, before they have learnt how to cope with it, their anger and aggression will grow and get more and more out of control. Anger needs to be 'managed' and expressed in a reasonably controlled way. There are even some occasions when it is in a child's best interest to keep feelings of anger under check – for example, when with a teacher or other person in authority.

Suppressing angry feelings only stores up problems for later on

Yes, suppression of anger is not a good idea. It is neverthe-less important that children learn to manage their anger so that it can be expressed at the right time and without getting out of control. But, as mentioned above, there are a few times when it is just not worth showing anger, when it would only make things worse. Children have to learn when these times are and how to first recognize anger and then to use the unexpressed anger in a constructive way.

'If anger is not brought out into the open, it is stored up and comes out some other way'

Not necessarily. Anger and other moods don't behave like physical forces and they don't obey the laws of physics. Very strong anger that is only expressed in a mild way, may not leave a store of anger if it is dealt with immediately, before it is allowed to get out of control. Sometimes it is possible for anger to just fade away over a period of time. On the other hand, a small amount of anger that is allowed to fester, may gradually build up and eventually come to the surface over some very insignificant event and be quite out of proportion.

'My mother says I grew out of my temper without her having to do anything, so why should I worry about my daughter's tempers'

Your mother may be right, but make your own decision and do what you think is right for *your* child. The danger of doing nothing is that your child may never learn how to control her temper and by the time you find this out it may be too late to do much about it.

'I have done everything you say . . . but it doesn't work!'

Well done! It is difficult to stick to doing the right thing all the time and to be consistent, but if that is what you are doing, keep at it and it will work in the end. The guidelines that I have given are tried and tested and can be expected to be successful if applied in a consistent and determined way. If you have done all this for several months without any improvement then something is wrong somewhere. Maybe all your hard work is being undermined by another person or perhaps your child really is very difficult. Think about it carefully, discuss it with a friend, read the book again and if you are still stuck, this is the time to get some professional help.

'I hardly agree with anything you have said'

Well, everybody is entitled to their own views! I have already said that there are a wide range of ideas about childcare and many different ways of bringing children up. There is no 'best way' because each individual has different needs. What works with one family may not work with another. I have tried to outline what the main issues are and what the mechanisms are, so that you can work out the details for yourself as they apply to your own situation. If your children are still young it is possible to make lots of mistakes without too much of an immediate effect on them. It is later on, as the children approach adolescence that any earlier mistakes in child-rearing tend to become more obvious.

The ideas and guidlines in this book are based on a lot of people's experience and the results of research. All I can say is that the approach described here is more likely to work with most children than any other.

What if . . .

'My son says I am unfair because other parents give lots of sweets and treats'

It sounds as though your son is good at persuasion and has learnt how to use words rather than tempers to get his own way. You should be pleased with yourself! However, if you follow what your child claims other parents do, you could soon get into a muddle – partly because it may not be true and partly because the other parents may have got it wrong. You should do what you feel is right for your child and not do something just because other parents do it. It is a good idea to teach your child right from the start that what other parents allow their children to do is irrelevant as far as you are concerned. What matters is what happens to your family and *you* decide what the rules are rather than your son.

'We don't agree with each other about how to cope with our daughter's tempers'

When parents don't agree on how to deal with tempers, each will cancel the effect of the other and there is little point in trying to do anything about the tempers until you can agree. Usually one parent takes a tougher line and the other a softer one. The stricter parent tries to be a bit tougher to compensate for the other's softness, but then the easy-going parent becomes even more indulgent to balance the effect of the other being too strict. In this way the parents' attitudes become polarized and what began as a slight difference between the parents grows into a big one and agreement is difficult if not impossible to reach.

It is vital that you reach some agreement. Otherwise the whole family will suffer. It would probably be best to try and reach a compromise, but if this is not possible then one of you will need to make the main decisions and the other will just have to go along with it and be prepared to back up the decision maker. Either one or both of you will have to change.

'I can't even control my *own* anger'

We all find it difficult, but somehow or other you will have to learn to control it, otherwise there is little chance of

your child controlling his or her temper. As you might have guessed, almost all the things that I have said about tempers and anger apply to adults as well. So you can work on it together!

'I can't avoid some situations that I know cause my daughter to have a temper'

It would never be possible to avoid all situations that cause tempers and it would not be a good idea anyway. Children have to learn to cope with frustration. At least you will know in advance which situations to watch out for and, if you plan in advance, things should not get too out of hand. It might even be a good idea to deliberately set up a situation where you know your daughter is at risk of a temper and help her to cope with it by talking about it before, during and after the event. This may sound a bit cold and technical, but at least you are helping your daughter to learn about the management of anger and if she is successful you can both celebrate!

'The distractions and warnings have stopped working'

Try some others! As children develop and change, so should your response to them. But you are quite right – as children grow up they become more difficult to distract away from whatever they intend to do. So you have to rely increasingly on all the hard work you have done with your child in earlier years. Certainly you will have to be careful that your distractions don't become more and more exciting or your child will soon learn how to work the system! At the same time, if you find that your warnings are becoming increasingly severe, it is time to review why your child is not learning how to manage anger.

'My son continues to sulk for hours after a temper'

Sulking is to a large extent part of a child's temperament and, like other aspects of personality, it is possible to 'shape' and change it to some degree. Teaching children to apologize helps to stop bad moods carrying on. If your son continues sulking in spite of everything, then it is best to take no notice at all and act as if things are quite normal. If all else fails, try tickling! It is important to set a good example for your son and make sure that he sees you dealing with your anger quickly and not letting it drag on. Don't forget other members of the family, because if they are good at sulking they will undermine all your hard work.

'I worry that my four-year-old son will harm himself because his tempers are so violent'

Some tempers can be quite frightening, but remember that tempers usually stop if there is no audience. A few children do have very bad tempers, but screaming and shouting will not do them any harm – it only exhausts them. No bad thing perhaps! Occasionally children deliberately hurt themselves during a temper to show everybody how serious it is. Biting and headbanging is not unusual.

In most cases this type of self-injury fades away quickly, once children realize that they are not getting attention or any other form of reward for this behaviour. Therefore, it is best to ignore your son should he start to hurt himself during a temper. Easier said than done, of course, but with a bit of advance planning and thought it should be possible. If your child were much older than four years of age, then self-injury would be more serious. This is partly because it indicates that anger is not under control and partly because it is much more likely that the child is in a seriously distressed state.

'My son breath-holds in a temper'

This is not unusual for young children, either at the beginning, or at the end of a temper. The child may go red, white or blue; he may go stiff or floppy, but after a few seconds he will start breathing again. Children normally grow out of this by the age of four or five years, and the less fuss you make of it the better. Breath-holding can be very frightening the first time you see it, but ordinary breath-holding associated with a temper is self-limiting – it will stop more quickly if you do nothing about it.

Sometimes it is even possible for breath-holding to lead to unconsciousness and there may be twitching of the arms and legs. Don't panic. If it is caused by the temper, the less you do the better. Rarely, this can be caused by an epileptic fit. Fits are not usually associated with tempers and the unconsciousness continues for longer than with the breath-holding. Get medical advice if you are in any doubt.

'My daughter is sometimes sick during a temper'

This is not unusual in young children and there is a danger that they will realize that it is a good way of getting attention and do it again. For this reason it is best to clear it up, giving as little attention to your daughter as possible, apart from a comment like 'How disgusting' or 'What a mess', depending on how deliberate you feel the vomiting was.

Parents worry that their child may inhale the vomit, but the risk of this is very small. If the child is still screaming with temper after being sick, there should be no reason to worry. But, if there is silence and your child is known to be sick easily, then it is worthwhile checking that all is well. Try to do this with as little attention to the child as possible.

'My child is too strong to hold in a temper'

Most parents can cope with holding a child up to the age of about five years old. At this age the worst of tempers should be over. Remember, never attempt to hold a child who is in a temper unless you are confident that you are strong enough to see it right to the end – when the child has calmed down and has apologized.

'I have done everything you have suggested – and more – but I really can't sort things out on my own. I think I need some professional help'

It is always difficult to know when it is the right time to get professional help with a family problem and even more difficult to know where to go and who to ask. Here are some suggestions:

- a lot will depend on the local services, so the first thing to do is to find out about them. You can do this through your local Library, Social Services Office or the Citizen's Advice Bureau. This will give you a list of agencies who provide help for parents, but it won't tell you how good the services are
- ask other parents and professionals what they know of the local services, but take what they say with a pinch of salt, because individual opinions may be unreliable – one of the best informed people is likely to be your GP
- voluntary groups for parents can be very supportive and give you an idea of how other people have coped, but they don't give professional advice, although they should be able to advise on how to get this type of help
- there is a wide range of professional groups who have specialized training and wide experience with children's emotional and behavioural problems, including

the following:
- paediatricians
- some social workers
- health visitors
- educational psychologists
- clinical psychologists
- child psychotherapists
- other child therapists
- some teachers
- children's nurses
- child psychiatrists

The difference between these various professions is confusing to say the least. One way round this problem is to ask your GP to refer you to the local Child Psychiatry Service where it is usual for some or all of the above professions to work closely together

- don't be put off a referral to the Child Psychiatry Service, if you feel the problem is beyond you. As a rule of thumb they are interested in helping any problem of emotions or behaviour that seem to be getting out of control and out of proportion to what might be expected in any given circumstances.

POSTSCRIPT

Now that you have come to the end of the book I hope you have found that you understand your child's anger better than before and that you are now able to work out what needs to be done if your child has a temper or becomes angry. Most important of all, you should know when anger is normal and when *not* to worry!

There may be parts of the book that you don't understand or that you disagree with. If this is the case, why not discuss it with several of your friends and see what they think?

Please don't feel guilty if you have found that you are doing something wrong. Unfortunately, an inevitable part of being a parent is feeling guilty and getting things wrong. We all do it! No parent has ever managed to get everything right all the time, so all that can be expected of us is that we try our best.

In fact, childcare is more about striking a delicate balance between what is best for the child and the needs of other members of the family, than doing the right thing all the time. Most parents follow their intuition and do 'what comes naturally'. The chances are that this will work well most of the time, but not always. It is for these times, when things aren't going smoothly that this book should be helpful and provide you with a few new ideas and guidelines to follow.

Finally, the love and affection that you have for your child will help you through the most difficult times, but do remember that one way of showing your love is to be firm and clear about how you expect your child to behave. Young children need this firmness and consistency in order to develop a feeling of security and confidence. As children grow older, the firmness can be gradually relaxed, but the consistency of care, affection and individual attention remain the essential ingredients of successful and happy childcare.

APPENDIX

WHAT THE RESEARCH SHOWS

Recent research has identified the main factors that are associated with tempers and anger in children. Not all of you will be interested in this and some will think, quite rightly, 'Research is not much use when my child is having a temper in the middle of a supermarket.' This is why the main part of the book deals with practical ways of coping with anger and understanding the many factors that cause tempers.

No doubt some of you will want to know something about the research on anger so that you can know what is normal and what areas you might like to read more about. I have selected some of the more relevant research studies of tempers and anger and given the references so that you can read the originals for yourself. Although some of the older research may seem a bit out of date, the studies I have chosen are now regarded as very important, classic studies.

Much of our everyday understanding of anger stems from the work of the psychoanalysts. Freud, Jung, Klein and others highlighted the importance of anger as a normal, and sometimes unconscious, motivating force. A great deal has been written about the psychoanalytic view of the child, who is portrayed as being at the mercy of unconscious aggressive and pleasure-seeking impulses. This view may seem compelling, and it has shaped the way many people understand anger in children, but unfortunately there is little or no research evidence that supports it. In fact, psychoanalytic theory is impossible to prove or disprove because it is based on assumptions about the unconscious mind which are, by their very nature, untestable.

Surveys

A better understanding of children's moods and tempers has come from a number of important surveys of young children. Most surveys use parental questionnaires and some also use reports from teachers and/or direct observation of the children. Each survey has some weaknesses in the way the research was carried out, but many of the findings have been confirmed time and time again and it is now possible to be quite confident about the results.

F. L. Goodenough (1931) was the first to carry out a detailed survey of tempers. She observed a large group of American children aged from one to seven years and also persuaded their mothers to keep a daily diary of the children's behaviour. Tempers were found to occur more often at bedtime, at the end of the morning and the end of the afternoon. It was assumed that these were the times when the children were hungry or tired.

After the age of two years the tempers gradually became shorter and less violent, but whining and sulking increased. Overall, the main cause for tempers was attempts to get the children to conform to accepted standards of social behaviour and relationships.

Subsequent surveys by J. W. Macfarlane et al (1954) in California and Naomi Richman (1977) in Waltham Forest, North London, confirmed F. L. Goodenough's findings that tempers are frequent in children aged from two to five years with a peak around two to three years old. Naomi Richman also reported that tempers and difficult behaviour are more common in boys than in girls and that difficult behaviour tends to persist. In fact, about 70 per cent of the children who had significant behaviour problems at three years of age still had them a year later.

In the same study, Naomi Richman found that the following family and social factors were associated with behaviour problems in the child:

- marital difficulties
- maternal depression
- large family size
- living in rented accommodation.

The British Births Survey followed up all the children born on or between the 5th and 11th April 1970. Using data collected when the children were five years of age, Jean Golding and D. Rush (1986) reported that 40 per cent of four to five year olds had tempers, of which 13 per cent had tempers at least once a week. Overall, boys had more temper tantrums than girls. Frequent tempers were more likely to occur if the children:

- had young or elderly mothers
- came from single-parent households
- came from step-parent households
- had poor social conditions
- were growing up with poverty and unemployment
- came from a household of more than three children
- had mothers who smoked heavily
- were living in an inner city area
- were living in the Midlands or North of England
- had a low birth-weight

Children with temper tantrums were also more likely to have the following problems:

- bed-wetting
- soiling
- feeding problems as a baby
- sleeping problems as a baby
- hyperactive

- generally difficult
- miserable
- speech and language difficulties
- headaches and stomach aches
- frequent sore throats and wheezing

The above are lists of statistically significant associations and they must be interpreted with care. For example, the link between tempers and mothers who smoke heavily may be a direct one of the effect of inhaled cigarette smoke on the child or it may be the effect of a difficult child causing the mother to smoke more. Alternatively the link might be an indirect one, such as poor living conditions, which could cause stress reactions in the child, causing tempers and, in the mother, leading to heavy smoking. Usually the links are due to many different factors, each interacting with the several others in a very complicated way.

Two other epidemiological surveys – one in Buckinghamshire (Professor Michael Shepherd et al 1971) and the other in the Isle of Wight (Professor Michael Rutter et al 1970) looked at older children who were attending school and found that tempers and aggression were still quite common, especially in boys. Professor Shepherd et al noted that 10 per cent of five-year-old boys had temper tantrums at least once a week, but the same frequency of tempers was only reported in 2 per cent of 15 year olds. However, irritability and other forms of angry behaviour tended to continue. It would seem that, although tempers tend to decrease with age, there is no evidence that children's experience of anger diminishes in any way – it just changes the way in which it shows itself.

The Isle of Wight and the Buckinghamshire surveys found that reports of children's moodiness and feelings of misery tended to increase in frequency as the children grew older. Of 10-11 year olds, 12 per cent felt miserable and this had doubled by the age of 14-15 years of age. So, while anger becomes less obvious, depression becomes more apparent.

Temperament

A very important longtitudinal study of young children in New York was reported by Alexander Thomas and Stella Chess (1977). They looked at nine temperamental characteristics and noted that the following were associated with an increased frequency of difficult behaviour, including tempers and irritability:

- **irregular eating and sleeping habits**
- **strong, mostly negative moods**
- **slow to adapt to new situations.**

Similar findings were reported by Professor Philip Graham et al (1973) in London. They identified a temperamental adversity index, using the above characteristics. The index was able to predict those children who were likely to have problems a year later. A high score gave a three-fold increase in the risk of difficult behaviour at home and an eight-fold risk of problems at school.

It is unclear how many of these characteristics are aspects of temperament, but it is clear that some children have certain characteristics in the make up of their personality that are present from an early age and which tend to persist. The above characteristics indicate a vulnerability to a wide range of behaviour problems, including tempers and tantrums.

One example of this vulnerability is the finding of Judy Dunn and others (1981) in Cambridge, that children with adverse temperamental characteristics were more likely to react badly to the birth of a sibling. Judy Dunn (1977) also noted that the same group of children were more likely to have accidents.

It is probable that it is not just a case of children behaving in a particular way because they have a certain type of temperament. It is more likely to be an interaction between the children and their environment, most notably the mother.

Angry behaviour

Apart from the early work on tempers, there is not much research that looks specifically at the angry behaviour of children as they grow older, the focus is more on overt aggression rather than anger. Of course there is a close link between the two emotions: anger is about the frustration of not having your own way, but aggression is more concerned with damage to people or property and is not always associated with anger.

A recent interesting study from the USA by E. M. Cummings et al (1984) investigated how children reacted to anger between their parents. Toddlers commonly reacted with distress and anger – even if the parent's anger was simulated. On the other hand, school-age children reacted more frequently by comforting or intervening in the argument. Some children consistently reacted more than others and this continued to be the case over a period of five years.

Children's responses to affection between their parents were also studied, and angry, distressed behaviour was again noted, although the main reaction was one of pleasure or seeking affection themselves. Interestingly, it was noted that angry incidents were reported two or three times more commonly than episodes of affection. This study supports the notion that parental behaviour is important in determining how their children feel and behave.

H. C. Dawe (1934) analysed 200 quarrels between 40 preschool children in a day-nursery and found the following:

- boys were more aggressive than girls
- most of the arguments were about possessions
- children tended to argue less as they grew older
- children became more aggressive as they grew older
- the average number of quarrels was three to four per hour

- most arguments were very short-lived, lasting about 20 seconds
- most arguments were sorted out by the children and caused little or no resentment.

The finding that angry quarrels are so frequent and brief at this young age is interesting, and, although the study was carried out a few years ago, there is no reason to think that children have changed much.

Conclusion

Research findings are a bit like a jigsaw puzzle: each piece of information may be the missing part you have been looking for, or it may not fit at all. I have outlined some of the main findings that fit together to make up a picture of tempers and anger. There are, however, many other research studies that are not so directly relevant, which help to complete the picture. You will already know some of this information or will come across it in the future. See how it fits into your own 'jigsaw' of tempers and anger. Don't throw information out if it doesn't immediately fit – there may be a place for it that you discover later.

I doubt if all the information in this book will fit into your own view of anger, but, just like the research information, try and keep it in your mind and, at a later date, you may be surprised to find how well it all fits together!

References

Cummings, E. M., Zahn-Waxler, C., and Radke-Yarrow, M., Developmental changes in children's reactions to anger in the home, (1984), J. Child Psychol. Psychiatry, 25, 63-74

Dawe, H. C., An analysis of 200 quarrels of pre-school children, (1934), Child Development, 6, 139-157

Dunn, J. F., Patterns of early interactions: continuities and consequences, *Studies in Mother-Infant Interactions*,

H. R. Shaffer, (Ed), Academic Press (1977)

Dunn, J. F., Kendrick, C., and MacNamee, R., The reaction of first-born children to the birth of a sibling: mothers' reports, (1981), J. Child Psychol. Psychiatry, 22, 1-18

Golding, J., Rush, D., Temper tantrums and other behaviour problems, *From Birth to Five*, A study of the health and behaviour of Britain's five year olds, N. Buttler and J. Golding, (Eds), Pergamon Press (1986)

Goodenough, F. L., Anger in young children, (1931), *Institute Child Welfare Monograph Series*, No 9, University of Minnesota Press, Minneapolis

Graham, P., Rutter, M., and George, S., Temperamental characteristics as predictors of behaviour problems in children, (1973) Amer. J. Orthopsychiatry, 43, 328-339

MacFarlane, J. W., Allen, L., and Honzicc, M. P., *A Developmental Study of the Behaviour Problems of Normal Children Between Twenty-one Months and Fourteen Years*, University of California Press, Berkely and Los Angeles, (1954)

Richman, N., Behaviour problems in pre-school children: family and social factors, (1977), Brit. J. Psychiatry, 131, 523-527

Rutter, M., Tizard, J., and Whitmore, K. (Eds) *Education Health and Behaviour*, Longman (1970)

Shepherd, M., Oppenheim, B., and Mitchell, S. *Childhood Behaviour and Mental Health*, University of London Press, (1971)

Thomas, A., and Chess, S. *Temperament and Development*, Brunner/Mazel (1977)

FURTHER READING

Ciba Foundation Symposium 80, *Temperamental Differences in Infants and Young Children*, Pitman (1982)
A helpful collection of papers presented at a symposium of world authorities on temperament.

Klama, John, *Aggression*, Conflict in animals and humans reconsidered, Longman Scientific and Technical (1988)
A thought-provoking book by a number of experts, looking at the nature of anger and aggression.

Herbert, Martin, *Conduct Disorders of Childhood and Adolescence*, A social learning perspective, John Wiley (1987)
A very detailed and technical book.

Rutter, Michael (Ed.), *Scientific Foundations of Developmental Psychiatry*, Heineman Medical Books (1980)
An excellent reference book on the wider aspects of child development.

INDEX